THE SHANG DYNASTY

BY GEORGE COTTRELL

KidHaven
PUBLISHING

Published in 2017 by
KidHaven Publishing, an Imprint of Greenhaven Publishing, LLC
353 3rd Avenue
Suite 255
New York, NY 10010

Designer: Natalie Carr
Editor: Grace Jones

Cataloging-in-Publication Data

Names: Cottrell, George.
Title: The Shang Dynasty / George Cottrell.
Description: New York : KidHaven Publishing, 2017. | Series: Unlocking ancient civilizations | Includes index.
Identifiers: ISBN 9781534520370 (pbk.) | ISBN 9781534520394 (library bound) | ISBN 9781534520387 (6 pack) | ISBN 9781534520400 (ebook)
Subjects: LCSH: China–History–Shang dynasty, 1766-1122 B.C.–Juvenile literature.
Classification: LCC DS744.C68 2017 | DDC 931'.02–dc23

Printed in the United States of America

CPSIA compliance information: Batch #CW17KL: For further information contact Greenhaven Publishing LLC, New York, New York at 1-844-317-7404.

Please visit our website, www.greenhavenpublishing.com. For a free color catalog of all our high-quality books, call toll free 1-844-317-7404 or fax 1-844-317-7405.

PHOTO CREDITS

THE SHANG DYNASTY

CONTENTS

All words that appear like *this* are explained in the glossary on page 31.

THE SHANG DYNASTY

THE Shang Dynasty was one of the most important *civilizations* in the history of the world. Even today, the *legacy* of the Shang can be seen in Chinese *society* and beyond.

It has helped create the structure of modern-day China and its influence can be seen in China's culture, politics, and geography to this day.

THE MODERN SITE OF THE SHANG CITY OF YIN, WHICH IS NEAR THE CITY OF ANYANG IN NORTHEASTERN CHINA

Although *historians'* opinions differ, it is generally thought that the *reign* of the Shang Dynasty began over 3,600 years ago, starting in 1600 BC and ending in 1050 BC. These dates also mark the period of the Chinese Bronze Age. The Bronze Age was a period in history noted for the use of the metal bronze in everyday life to make objects such as *vessels*, jewelry, and weapons. It was also the first time the written word was used.

THIS IS AN EXAMPLE OF A BRONZE AGE CUP THAT MAY HAVE BEEN USED FOR RELIGIOUS RITUALS OR FOR DRINKING.

THE BEGINNINGS OF THE SHANG DYNASTY

Most historians agree that the Shang Dynasty began when Tang of Shang defeated Jie at the Battle of Mingtiao in around 1600 BC. Jie was the leader of the Xia, the previous ruling dynasty. With his victory, Tang became known as King Tang and promised to create a dynasty that would bring success and happiness to the people he now ruled over.

WHAT IS A DYNASTY?

A dynasty is a period of time when people from the same family rule one after the other.

A MODERN STAMP WITH A DRAWING OF WHAT KING TANG MAY HAVE LOOKED LIKE

THE WRITTEN WORD WAS FIRST USED AND RECORDED DURING THE SHANG DYNASTY. EXAMPLES OF EARLY SHANG WRITING LIKE THIS, WHICH HAVE BEEN CARVED ON BONE, HELP US UNDERSTAND THE HISTORY OF THE SHANG.

Under the rule of King Tang, the people of the Shang Dynasty saw their lives improve. A society began to grow that brought more wealth to the dynasty and, for a civilization of the time, treated *peasants* well.

A GROWING DYNASTY

THIS period of calm and development carried on for around 200 years until the ninth king, Tai Wu, ended his reign. It was during this time that the Shang entered the Bronze Age and began to produce many of the bronze objects that have since been found at **archaeological** sites across modern-day China.

A BRONZE VESSEL MADE BY THE SHANG

After the reign of Tai Wu, the Shang Dynasty entered a time of chaos. It was affected by fighting between members of the royal family, a growing number of enemies, and social problems had started to occur, such as the unfair treatment of peasants.

The problems of the Shang ended when Pan Geng, the 19th king, came to rule. Seeing how Shang society had become increasingly worse, he reintroduced a style of leadership that was much more similar to King Tang's. He introduced a number of **reforms** and greatly improved the lives of peasants. As a result, he oversaw a period of happiness and success for the Shang Dynasty.

A STONE CARVING OF THE LAST SHANG KING, DI XIN

THE END OF THE SHANG

In around 1050 BC, King Wu, a rival leader of the *Zhou*, defeated the last Shang king, Di Xin, at the Battle of Muye. This marked the end of the Shang Dynasty and the beginning of the Zhou Dynasty which continued to reign for the next 700 years.

ORACLE BONES

ORACLE bones have been key in helping historians understand the Shang Dynasty. Made of bone or turtle or tortoise shell, they were used by the Shang to try to predict the future. They would ask the gods and their **ancestors** about things such as the weather, harvests, or fortunes of royal family members by carving the questions onto the oracle bones.

THESE ORACLE BONES WERE FOUND AT THE LOCATION OF THE SHANG CITY OF YIN.

HOW DID THE SHANG USE ORACLE BONES?

When they had carved the questions onto the oracle bones, heat would be applied to them until they cracked from the pressure. A *diviner* would interpret these cracks in order to provide answers to the questions they had carved. The answers would then also be carved onto the oracle bones.

Oracle bones mark the beginning of Chinese written history. They have allowed historians to find out more about the period, especially about the Shang people's beliefs and the religion that they may have followed. Before the discovery of oracle bones some historians even questioned the existence of the Shang Dynasty.

A SITE AT THE RUINS OF YIN, WHERE OVER 20,000 ORACLE BONES HAVE BEEN FOUND

DISCOVERING THE ORACLE BONES

The oracle bones of the Shang Dynasty were first discovered in the early 20th century at the site of the Shang city, Yin, near present-day Anyang. These first discoveries uncovered over 20,000 oracle bones, which allowed historians to learn about the culture of the Shang people as well as what their day-to-day lives might have been like.

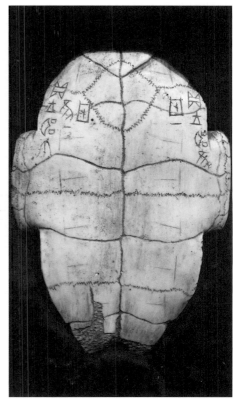

EVERYDAY LIFE

DURING the Shang Dynasty, people experienced improvements in their living conditions and day-to-day lives.

Although people continued to live off the land, they stopped living as **nomads** and began to settle on farms and in villages, towns, and cities.

THE SKULL OF A PERSON FROM THE SHANG DYNASTY

FARMING

Farming was very important to the people of the Shang. As the dynasty was located in the Yellow River valley, the Shang people were able to develop ways to stop flooding while, at the same time, helping to water their crops. They mostly farmed crops such as millet, wheat, rice and barley. They also raised animals such as pigs, dogs, oxen, and even silkworms!

THE LIFE OF FARMERS

Although the majority of the Shang worked as farmers, they did not own the land that they worked on. Instead, they were given a small area of land by the *noblemen* who owned it. In return, the farmers would offer some of their crops to them and work for free on the noblemen's homes or on the land that they owned.

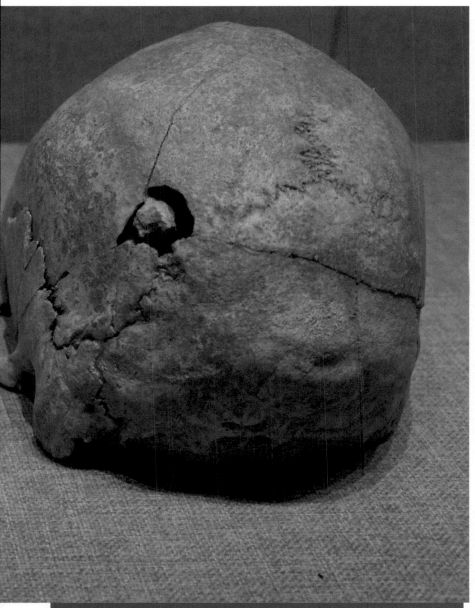

Farmers and their families would have lived near the land that they farmed. Their houses would have been simple buildings made out of mud or bamboo and would have housed the entire family.

A JADE KNIFE THAT PEOPLE WOULD HAVE USED FOR CUTTING OBJECTS AS PART OF THEIR DAY-TO-DAY LIVES

FAMILY LIFE

Men and women had clear and very different roles within everyday family life. In Shang society, men were seen as leaders and had control over their families. Normally, the eldest male was the head of the family.

THIS IS A BRONZE COOKING VESSEL. BRONZE ITEMS LIKE THIS WERE TOO EXPENSIVE FOR EVERYONE EXCEPT THE WEALTHIEST FAMILIES.

The role of women was also clear in Shang society and very different to that of a man's. Wives had to obey and respect their husbands at all times. However, women did not normally choose their own husband. Instead, this was done by their fathers.

WAR AND PEACE

Of the many things that oracle bones have told us about the Shang Dynasty, one of the clearest is that Shang kings were often at war with nearby *tribes* and kingdoms. However, when there was peace, the Shang developed *trading routes* within their kingdom. This allowed them to bring new technology, such as the horse-drawn chariot, from western Asia.

The Shang's superior weapons meant that they often won battles. The weapons that they used included the bronze-tipped halberd as well as bows and arrows. The Shang created their armies by forcing peasant farmers to fight for their *warlords*.

A BRONZE HELMET THAT WOULD HAVE BEEN WORN BY A SHANG SOLDIER

A halberd is a mixture of spear and axe. During the Shang Dynasty, it was made out of an axe head placed on a long pole and was a successful weapon for the Shang. The picture to the right shows a bronze halberd from the Shang Dynasty.

ART AND CULTURE

AS the Shang Dynasty grew in size and wealth, so did the quality of the art and culture that it was producing. Some of the most popular products were delicate musical instruments, jade jewelry, bronze vessels, and finely woven silk cloth.

Many of these items have been found at nearly all of the Shang Dynasty archaeological sites in China, including modern-day Anyang in Northern China in 1928, the sites at Erligang near Zhengzhou in 1952, and Erlitou, near Luoyang, in 1959. These three sites and their *artifacts* have given historians an idea as to how the art and culture changed and became more advanced over time.

10.00
商父丙角
中華民國郵票
REPUBLIC OF CHINA

A MODERN STAMP THAT SHOWS WHAT A PIECE OF SHANG BRONZE WORK WOULD HAVE LOOKED LIKE

THIS IS A JADE VESSEL CALLED A CONG. HISTORIANS ARE UNSURE WHAT IT WAS USED FOR.

BRONZE WORK

The Shang, as archaeological discoveries have shown, were skilled workers who used many materials. Tools, **ornaments,** and jewelry from the period have been found made out of bone, jade, ceramic, stone, and wood. However, it is the use of bronze that the Shang are most known for.

HOW DID THEY DO IT?

The Shang were able to make such amazing bronze items because they used a method called piece-mold casting. They would heat bronze until it became a liquid and then pour it into a mold made of clay. Once cooled to a sufficient temperature, they would then remove the clay to reveal the bronze design inside.

Bronze was only available to a small number of people in Shang society because it was very expensive. Due to its strength, many of the bronze items produced during the Shang Dynasty have survived to this day. Lots of bronze was made into vessels to be used as part of burial or worship *rituals*. Later in the Shang Dynasty, bronze was also used to write on.

THE HOUMUWU DING

THE Houmuwu ding is a large piece of bronze work that shows the skill of bronze workers during the Shang Dynasty. Discovered in 1939 in Anyang, it is the largest piece of bronze work to survive from anywhere in the ancient world. It is believed to have been made as a ritual ding to be buried alongside royalty. Dings were vessels that stood upon legs and were used for cooking, storage or as part of rituals.

MUSIC AND THE XUN

Music was a major part of everyday life during the Shang Dynasty. The introduction of piece-mold casting allowed for more complex musical instruments to be made. Archaeologists have found several examples of instruments at Yin, including drums and Xuns, which are traditional Chinese *ocarinas*.

A XUN, SIMILAR TO THOSE FOUND AT THE SITE OF YIN

CITIES OF THE SHANG

The capital city was the place where the king lived and ruled from. It contained the *royal court* and would have been where important decisions about the kingdom were made. Historians think that the Shang capital often moved because of arguments between members of the royal family.

全国重点文物保护单位

郑州商代遗址

中华人民共和国国务院1961年3月4日 公布

河南省人民政府2011年1月1日 立

THIS PICTURE SHOWS A PART OF A SHANG CITY THAT WAS DISCOVERED IN 1950. SOME HISTORIANS BELIEVE IT IS THE FIRST SHANG CAPITAL, BO.

A KINGDOM OF CAPITALS

THROUGHOUT the reign of the Shang Dynasty there was always a capital city. The first of these was built at a place called Bo by King Tang. Although the capital city moved many times, most historians believe that certain cities, such as the Great City of Shang, remained important throughout the Shang Dynasty. This is because items relating to the royal family have been found in the *ruins* of the city.

The major cities of the Shang Dynasty were located in what is now northeastern China. Many of these cities were established in the valley of the Yellow River, including the city of Yin.

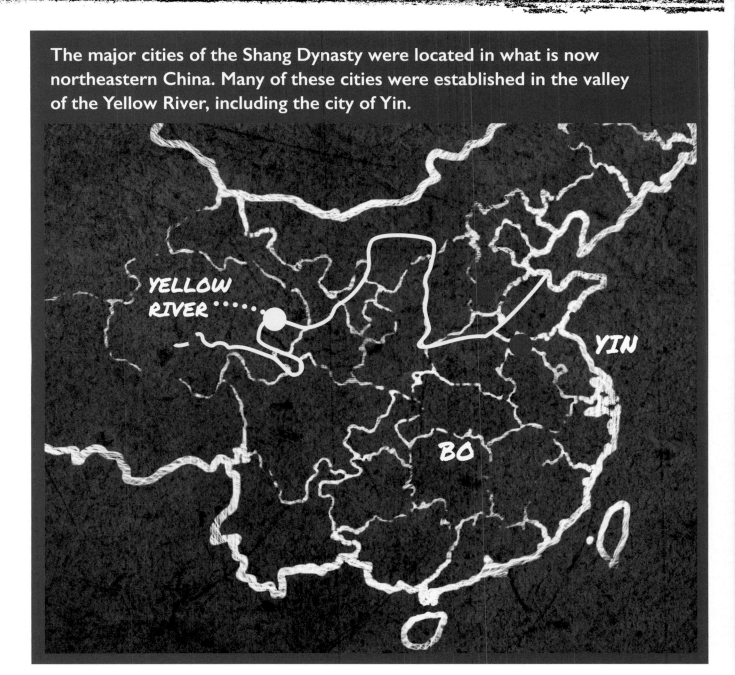

YELLOW RIVER

YIN

BO

Yin was the last capital city of the Shang Dynasty and one of its most important. In 1899, the ruins of the city were discovered and revealed many very important artifacts, including oracle bones, that taught us much about everyday life during the Shang Dynasty. Yin was founded in the late 1400s BC by King Pan Geng and remained the capital for 255 years until the fall of the Shang Dynasty.

THIS IS WHAT YIN LOOKS LIKE TODAY.

MONARCHS AND RULERS
A TRADITIONAL HIERARCHY

LIKE many other ancient civilizations, Shang society had a strict *hierarchy*. The king and his family were at the very top, followed by noblemen, who held roles in the government and army. Priests were next and then the *merchants*, craftsmen, and farmers.

THIS IS A PAINTING OF KING TANG, WHO WAS THE FIRST RULER OF THE SHANG.

A TIME OF KINGS

There were either 29 or 30 kings, across 17 different generations, during the reign of the Shang Dynasty. The last king was the much-hated Di Xin, who killed himself after losing the Battle of Muye. Di Xin was hated because of his cruel treatment of peasants and poor management of the Shang's wealth.

1

2

3

4

KING TANG

King Tang was the founder and first ruler of the Shang Dynasty. He did much to help his people and to develop Shang society. Known as a kind and gentle king, his people loved him and saw their kingdom succeed under his rule.

KING WU DING (1250 BC – 1192 BC)

King Wu Ding, whose reign lasted for around 50 years, was the longest serving of all of the Shang kings. He helped to bring peace to the Shang by not only defeating his enemies, but by also marrying women from rival tribes in order to create new, peaceful relationships with them.

THE SHANG HIERARCHY

1. THE KING

2. NOBLEMEN

3. PRIESTS

4. MERCHANTS, CRAFTSMEN, AND FARMERS

THE SHANG DYNASTY ROYAL CEMETERY IN ANYANG

The home of simuwu ding

FU HAO

THE LIFE OF FU HAO

FU Hao is a unique character in the history of the Shang. As one of King Wu Ding's 60 wives, she became an important figure in a time when usually only men had power.

When the Shang Dynasty was at its strongest, Fu Hao became not only a wife but a military leader, politician, and *priestess*.

THE TOMB OF FU HAO

In 1976, the tomb of Fu Hao was uncovered near Anyang. It contained many artifacts, such as oracle bones, that helped historians learn just how much of an important figure Fu Hao was in Shang society.

When discovered, Fu Hao's tomb contained around 2,000 items. Of these items, 468 were made out of bronze, 750 out of jade, 560 out of bone, over 110 out of stone and semiprecious stones, and more than 100 were weapons.

A STATUE OF FU HAO

MILITARY LEADER

According to the writing on the oracle bones found near her tomb, Fu Hao led an army into battle several times, helping King Wu Ding defeat the Shang Dynasty's enemies, including their rivals, the Tu-Fang.

THIS IS THE TOMB OF FU HAO, NOW A FAMOUS HISTORICAL SITE.

A TRUSTED FIGURE

Such was King Wu Ding's confidence in Fu Hao that she was often involved in rituals and *sacrifices* – something never normally done by women in Shang society. These often involved killing animals or enemies of the Shang to please the gods. The size and beauty of her tomb, built by Wu Ding, helped tell historians how important she was.

RELIGION
HOW RELIGIOUS WERE THE SHANG?

FOR the Shang, religion played a major role in everyday life. Everyone in Shang society was religious because the Shang believed that failure to worship the gods would lead to disaster for their families and the kingdom.

THIS IS A JADE CONG THAT PROBABLY WOULD HAVE BEEN USED FOR RELIGIOUS RITUALS.

HOW DID THE SHANG WORSHIP?
The Shang believed that there were many different gods who controlled various parts of life, such as the sun, wind, rain, and other natural forces. They also gave great importance to the worship of their ancestors, who they believed still existed after death and could help them from the *afterlife*. They would show their strong belief in ancestor worship by performing rituals and sacrifices.

SHANG DI

One god, called Shang Di, was considered to be the most powerful god. He controlled the other gods of nature and was the link to ancestors in the afterlife. Therefore, people made sure to worship him regularly.

THIS VESSEL FEATURES A TAOTIE. A TAOTIE IS A DESIGN THAT LOOKS LIKE A MONSTER AND APPEARED ON MANY OF THE VESSELS USED FOR RELIGIOUS RITUALS.

Death was treated very seriously in Shang society and linked closely to religion. Due to their beliefs, people were buried with objects that they thought would be useful to them in the afterlife. Important people in Shang society often had elaborate stone tombs made for them that contained hundreds of objects such as weapons, jewelry, and even the bodies of their servants.

THE LEGACY OF THE SHANG

THE Shang Dynasty introduced many new ideas and technologies. One invention was the written word. Modern Chinese writing has developed directly from the form that the Shang used and many symbols used today are similar to those that the Shang first created.

A MODERN CHINESE ZODIAC WHEEL SHOWS HOW THE SHANG'S DISCOVERIES IN ASTRONOMY HAVE BEEN USED.

THE LUNAR CALENDAR

The beginnings of Chinese *astronomy* and the modern-day Chinese calendar were first recorded during the Shang Dynasty. Based on the moon's cycle, their calendar lasted 366 days and recognized other key events such as *solar eclipses*.

NUMBERING SYSTEM

The introduction of the written word in Shang society also allowed them to develop a complex numbering system. They were among the first civilizations to introduce a decimal system. Carvings on oracle bones dating to the 13th century BC show this. This system of numbers allowed the Shang to develop a monetary system far more advanced than the ancient Egyptians were using at the same point in history.

The Shang Dynasty was one of the most important ancient civilizations in both Chinese and world history. It marks the beginning of the period of the great dynasties in China and laid the foundations of a Chinese social system that still exists today.

2070–1600 BC

→

THE RULE OF THE XIA DYNASTY

1700s BC

→

THE BEGINNING OF THE MIDDLE BRONZE AGE

1600 BC

→

THE SHANG DYNASTY BEGINS AND KING TANG BEGINS HIS REIGN

1300s BC

→

THE CITY OF YIN IS FOUNDED

1250 BC

→

KING WU DING TAKES THE THRONE

1200 BC

→

FU HAO DIES

1192 BC

→

KING WU DING DIES

SHANG DYNASTY

1600 BC
→
THE FOUNDING OF THE FIRST CAPITAL, BO

1500s BC
→
THE REIGN OF KING TAI WU

1400s BC
→
THE REIGN OF KING PAN GENG

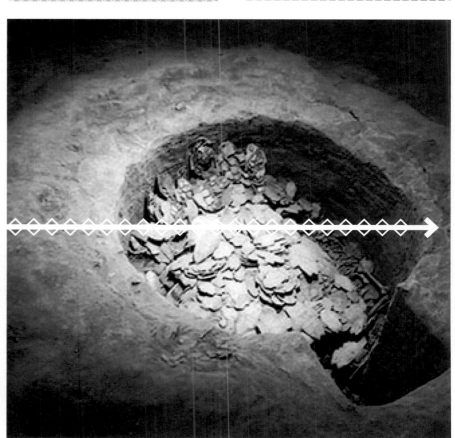

1200–1046 BC
→
THE SHANG DYNASTY STARTS TO WEAKEN

1046 BC
→
KING DI XIN LOSES THE THRONE

1046 BC
→
THE SHANG DYNASTY ENDS AND THE ZHOU DYNASTY BEGINS

MAP OF THE SHANG DYNASTY

BOUNDARY OF MODERN-DAY CHINA

SHANG DYNASTY

YELLOW RIVER   BEIJING

CHINA

YIN (ANYANG)

AO   BO

ZHOU STATE

SHANG DYNASTY

GLOSSARY

afterlife	a religious belief that there is life after death
ancestors	people who lived before someone they are related to
archaeological	related to the study of past humans and their cultures through old materials
artifacts	objects made by people, typically ones of cultural or historical interest
astronomy	the study of the universe
civilizations	societies that are very advanced
diviner	a person who tries to predict the future
generations	groups of people from the same family or society who are about the same age
hierarchy	a system where people are ranked in order of power or importance
historians	experts in the study of history
legacy	something handed down from one generation to the next
merchants	people involved in trading goods, often with other countries
noblemen	people who are part of the highest social class
nomads	people who do not live in one place
ocarinas	ancient wind instruments
ornaments	things used for decoration
peasants	poor land workers who belonged to the lowest social class
priestess	a female who carries out religious actions or leads religious ceremonies
reforms	to make changes to something in order to improve it
reign	the period of time a leader rules for
rituals	a series of ordered actions during a religious ceremony
royal court	the place where a royal leader mostly rules from
ruins	the remains of a structure or building
sacrifices	when animals or people are killed in order to try to please a god or religious figure
society	a group of people who live together in a community
solar eclipses	when the light of the sun is blocked by the moon
trading routes	links between cities and towns that allow goods to be transported
tribes	groups of people linked by family, social, religious or community ties
vessels	containers for food or drink
warlords	people who are powerful enough to gather and command an army
Zhou	the dynasty that followed the Shang

INDEX